EATING BUGS
AS SUSTAINABLE FOOD

BY CECILIA PINTO McCARTHY

CONTENT CONSULTANT
Bill Schindler
Director, Eastern Shore Food Lab; Associate Professor,
Anthropology, Washington College

Core Library

An Imprint of Abdo Publishing

Cover image: People around the world enjoy bugs

abdocorelibrary.com

Printed in the United States of America, North Mankato, Minnesota
032019
092019

THIS BOOK CONTAINS
RECYCLED MATERIALS

Cover Photo: Karina Urmantseva/iStockphoto
Interior Photos: Karina Urmantseva/iStockphoto, 1; Shutterstock Images, 4–5, 22–23, 30 (steer), 30 (mealworms); Red Line Editorial, 6; CK Bangkok Photography/Shutterstock Images, 9, 45; Jen Watson/Shutterstock Images, 12–13; Eppic Photography/iStockphoto, 14; Ihor Bondarenko/Shutterstock Images, 17; Sawat Banyenngam/Shutterstock Images, 18; Ton Koene/picture-alliance/dpa/AP Images, 27; Claudio Zaccherini/Shutterstock Images, 32–33, 43; Godong/Universal Images Group/Getty Images, 35; John Stillwell/PA Wire URN:17327937/Press Association/AP Images, 39

Editor: Marie Pearson
Series Designer: Ryan Gale

Library of Congress Control Number: 2018966159

Publisher's Cataloging-in-Publication Data

Names: McCarthy, Cecilia Pinto, author.
Title: Eating bugs as sustainable food / by Cecilia Pinto McCarthy
Description: Minneapolis, Minnesota : Abdo Publishing, 2020 | Series: Unconventional science | Includes online resources and index.
Identifiers: ISBN 9781532118999 (lib. bdg.) | ISBN 9781532173172 (ebook) | ISBN 9781644940907 (pbk.)
Subjects: LCSH: Entomophagy--Juvenile literature. | Insects as food--Juvenile literature. | Sustainable agriculture--Juvenile literature. | Environmental protection--Juvenile literature. | Food chains (Ecology)--Juvenile literature. | Food customs--Juvenile literature.
Classification: DDC 394.1--dc23

CONTENTS

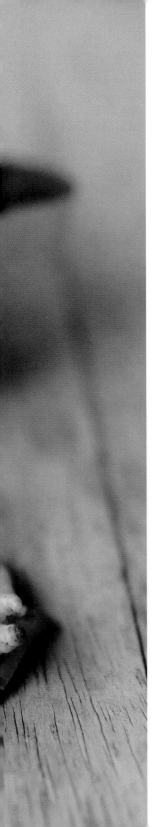

FOOD FOR A HUNGRY WORLD

Daniella Martin hosted a cooking and travel show. On the show's first episode, Martin prepares her special taco recipe. She heats olive oil in a frying pan. Then she adds chopped onions. They sizzle and brown in the hot oil. She removes the taco filling from the freezer and adds a cupful to the pan. After two minutes, dinner is ready. Martin spoons hot filling into a soft tortilla. Avocado slices and chopped tomatoes go on next. Finally, she sprinkles on cilantro and a dash of hot sauce. Martin takes

Some people enjoy dishes made with waxworms.

WHO EATS BUGS?

This map shows, by region, the number of countries where people frequently eat bugs. What continent has the most countries where people eat insects?

Europe

Asia

Africa

North and South America

Oceania

North and South America: 23 Countries
Europe: 11 Countries
Africa: 36 Countries
Asia: 29 Countries
Oceania: 14 Countries

a big bite of taco. As she does, waxworms tumble from the taco onto her plate.

Waxworms are wax moth caterpillars. Some people would be disgusted by a taco filled with waxworms. But Martin thinks waxworms are delicious. In fact, she thinks lots of bugs are tasty. Martin is an entomophagist, a person who eats insects. She has eaten more than two dozen kinds of bugs. She hopes that her cooking show will encourage others to eat bugs too.

WHAT DO BUGS TASTE LIKE?

Edible bugs have a range of flavors. Some taste like blends of familiar foods. Others, such as the giant water bug, have a unique flavor that people find hard to describe. When roasted, most insects taste nutty. Roasted crickets remind diners of nutty shrimp. Waxworms and bee larvae taste like mushrooms, nuts, and bacon. In Australia, honeypot ants are prized for the sugary liquid they carry in their swollen bellies. In sub-Saharan Africa, children collect termites after rainstorms. Boiled, salted termites are popular snacks. They taste like bits of crispy bacon.

YUMMY OR YUCKY?

Eating bugs is not a new fad. Ancient humans ate insects, plants, and animals. Locusts and beetles were part of ancient Greek and Roman diets. Bugs have been a staple food for people in Central and South America, Asia, and Africa for thousands of years. Today, 2 billion people around the world eat insects. In Mexico, children crunch toasted grasshoppers. A Thai dinner might include batter-fried giant water bugs served with sweet plum sauce.

BUGS IN EVERYDAY FOODS

People don't realize they eat bugs every day. It is impossible for every insect, larva, or egg to be removed from crops. They end up in packaged foods. Peanut butter, pizza sauce, and pasta can all have some insect parts and eggs. Some foods have insect ingredients that are added on purpose. Carmine is a natural red dye. It is made from crushed cochineal insects. Carmine gives some red velvet cake mixes, candies, and yogurts their red color.

There are many ways to prepare and enjoy eating bugs.

In North America and Europe, however, most people do not eat bugs. Many think bugs are dirty pests. Instead, Westerners get much of their protein from livestock such as cattle, pigs, and chickens.

FEEDING A GROWING POPULATION

Experts estimate that by 2050 the world population will reach 9 billion people. Food production would have to nearly double to feed so many people. Raising more livestock is not an option. Land for raising livestock is scarce. Oceans cannot provide enough food either. Oceans have been overfished. Changing global climates are also affecting food supplies. Extreme storms, flooding, and droughts make it difficult to raise livestock. Raising livestock also pollutes the environment.

Some people say that bugs are the solution. Insects reproduce quickly. They use little space, food, and water. They make very little waste. These characteristics make them cheap to raise in large quantities. Bugs are also nutritious. They are a great source of protein, good fats, vitamins, and minerals. Raising insects causes less pollution than raising livestock.

Attitudes about eating bugs are changing. Entomophagy, or eating bugs, is slowly becoming more acceptable in Western cultures. In the United States and Europe, there are several edible insect farms. They supply bugs to restaurants. They also make insect powders for protein shakes, cookies, and other snacks. Some candy stores sell chocolate-covered ants and cricket lollipops. Experts are improving ways to raise, harvest, and process bugs for food.

EXPLORE ONLINE

Chapter One mentions that insects are eaten in many countries. The website below goes into more depth on this topic. What new information did you learn from the website?

SCIENCE NEWS FOR STUDENTS: YUMMY BUGS
abdocorelibrary.com/bugs-sustainable-food-source

RUNNING OUT OF RESOURCES

I n 2016, the United Nations set 17 Sustainable Development Goals. The goals challenge countries to improve people's lives and protect the planet. One goal is "Zero Hunger." Its focus is ensuring that people around the world have enough food. It also stresses growing food in a way that does not harm the environment.

Current methods of food production will not make enough food for future generations. Also, large-scale agricultural practices are not sustainable. Sustainable practices are eco-friendly. They preserve resources such as land and water for future generations.

The way people currently raise and eat livestock such as cattle cannot meet the global demand for food.

Massive areas of forest are cleared for farming every year.

Large-scale farming uses up natural resources. It pollutes the air, land, and water. It destroys habitats. Raising animals for meat is a leading cause of plant and animal extinction.

TREES AND FISH

Every year, millions of acres of land are taken for agriculture. The United Nations estimates that half of the world's tropical forests have been cleared for agriculture. Approximately 70 percent of agricultural land is used to raise livestock.

Three billion people worldwide rely on oceans for food. But overfishing has reduced fish populations. Large commercial fishing

A NATURAL RESOURCE

Insect populations are natural resources just like land and water. Insects also face many of the same threats. Overharvesting insects from the wild reduces their numbers. Insect populations have decreased because of pollution, habitat destruction, and climate change. Wildfires, floods, and droughts kill bugs or force them to move. Scientists are learning how bugs interact with their environments. Understanding these interactions helps scientists protect insects and their habitats. For example, planting host trees provides food for caterpillars. They are able to produce more offspring. In some areas, restrictions limit the number, kind, or time of year that insects can be harvested.

fleets catch massive amounts of fish. When too many fish are taken, they don't have a chance to reproduce. Their numbers drop.

POLLUTING THE PLANET

Farming causes pollution. Farm machinery is powered by fuel. When fuel burns, it emits greenhouse gases. Greenhouse gases are important. They control Earth's temperature. They keep the planet warm. But human activities create extra amounts of greenhouse gases. The gases build up in the atmosphere. They trap too much heat. The rising temperature causes climate change.

Pesticides keep crops free of pests. Pests can destroy crops. Fertilizers help crops grow. But pesticides and fertilizers have harmful chemicals too. The chemicals seep into soil and water supplies. Fertilizers also have nitrogen and phosphorus. Too much nitrogen and phosphorus cause algae and other water plants to overgrow. Too much algae reduce oxygen in the water.

Too much algae can make it hard for fish to survive.

Fish cannot breathe. Some algae produce toxins and bacteria. The bacteria contaminate the water. This can make animals and people sick.

Approximately 45 percent of the land on Earth is covered by livestock. Livestock pollute land and water with their manure and urine. Animal waste has nitrogen

and phosphorus. Waste washes into nearby water sources. It creates dead zones. Dead zones have low levels of oxygen. Any animal life in these zones either dies or leaves. Farm animals also produce methane gas in their stomachs. Methane is a greenhouse gas. It contributes to climate change.

WATER AND FOOD

Approximately 70 percent of global fresh water goes toward watering crops. And the demand for water is expected to increase. By 2050, almost 90 percent of all fresh water taken from lakes and other sources will be used for crops. In addition, water is becoming more scarce. Population growth and overuse of water sources stress water supplies. Climate change also affects water. Many regions experience long periods of drought. In other areas, severe storms trigger floods. Torrential downpours damage water pipelines and pollute water sources.

Extreme weather can make it hard to grow crops.

GOOD NUTRITION

People in developing countries often lack enough good food. Many suffer from malnutrition. Rice is a main food for more than half of the world's people. It is a major part of diets in developing countries. But rice alone does not provide all the nutrients people need. One solution is to make rice into flour. The rice flour can be made more nutritious by adding bug flour to it. Cricket and locust flours add healthy protein. The flour blend can then be made into foods such as cereals and pasta.

The United Nations Food and Agriculture Organization works to end hunger. It estimates that 821 million people worldwide regularly do not get enough nutritious food. Poor nutrition causes serious health problems. Children suffer from stunted growth. They are weak and underweight. They get sick easily. Every year, about 3 million children die of malnutrition. As the world population increases, food becomes scarce. To feed the growing population, people need to rethink how they get their food.

STRAIGHT TO THE
SOURCE

In the following passage, writer Lisa Spear discusses
the impact that eating meat has on the planet:

> *A new analysis suggests that the rise in meat consumption,
> driven by population and income growth, could play a
> major role in increasing carbon emissions and reducing
> biodiversity. . . .*
>
> *The debate over the environmental consequences of eating meat
> is nothing new. It's already widely known that meat production
> creates far more pollution than bringing vegetables, fruits, and
> grains to market. . . .*
>
> *In 2014, a study found that giving up beef could reduce a
> person's carbon footprint more significantly than if they gave up
> their cars.*

Source: Lisa Spear. "Global Meat Production Is Growing at an
Unsustainable Pace," *Newsweek*. Newsweek, July 23, 2018.
Web. Accessed November 20, 2018.

What's the Big Idea?

Take a close look at this passage. How does eating
meat affect the environment? What does the author
say is fueling the increased consumption of meat?

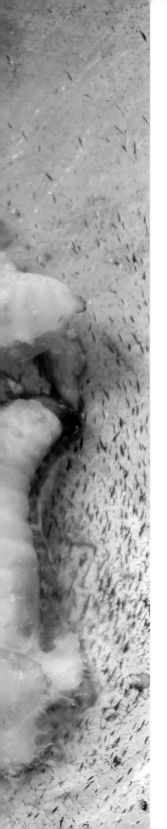

FROM PEST TO PLATE

Bugs are a plentiful food source. There are 2,100 types of edible bugs. Most come from the wild. The most commonly eaten insects are beetles. Many beetles are eaten as larvae. Larvae are immature forms of adult insects. Caterpillars, grubs, and maggots are larvae. One of the most popular edible insects is the palm weevil larva. It is found in tropical Africa, Asia, and South America.

Several types of butterflies, moths, and their caterpillars are edible. In southern Africa, approximately 9.5 billion mopane caterpillars are harvested for food every year. People in

Some people in Thailand eat seasoned palm weevil larva.

Thailand eat the bamboo caterpillar. People in Mexico eat at least 67 species of butterflies and moths. Wasps, bees, ants, termites, locusts, grasshoppers, and crickets are eaten around the world. In Japan, an annual festival showcases foods made from wasp larvae called hebo.

HEALTHY BUGS

The nutritional makeup of bugs varies. Adults usually have more protein than younger insects. An insect's diet and habitat can affect its nutritional value. Farm-raised grasshoppers fed on bran had almost twice as much protein as corn-fed grasshoppers. Roasting, frying, or boiling can also change an insect's nutrition. One study showed that dried mopane caterpillars had 9 percent more protein than roasted caterpillars. But overall, insects are a valuable source of nutrients.

Bugs have a lot of protein. Pound for pound, many insects have more protein than beef, pork, chicken, and fish. Protein is an important part of the human diet. Protein builds and maintains muscles, bones, skin, hair, and other tissues. It also powers body functions. Three and a half ounces (100 g) of mopane caterpillars have up to 1.2 ounces (35g) of protein. An equal amount of beef has 0.74 ounces (21 g) of protein.

Bugs are excellent sources of high-quality fat, fiber, vitamins, minerals, and other nutrients. House crickets have approximately 19 times more vitamin B2 than the same amount of beef. Just 3.5 ounces (100 g) of mopane caterpillars have five times more iron than the same amount of beef. Most insects are also high in fatty

INSECT FOOD ALLERGIES

Not much is known about allergic reactions to eating bugs. But research shows that people who are allergic to shellfish may also be allergic to bugs. Insects are closely related to some shellfish. Shrimp, crabs, and lobsters are all crustaceans. Shellfish are considered insects of the sea. People with shellfish allergies are more likely to be sensitive to the proteins in edible bugs. And allergy doctors suggest that people with allergies to bee venom avoid eating bees and wasps.

acids. Fats are especially important for malnourished children and adults. Insects are so nutritious because they are usually eaten whole. Their hard, outer skeletons and internal organs have vital minerals such as calcium. Insects can be fed special diets that boost their nutritional content. When researchers fed carrots to locusts, the insects gained more fat. They also had higher levels of beta-carotene. In the human body, beta-carotene is used to make vitamin A.

SAFER

Bugs are safer to eat than other types of meat. Viruses and bacteria that make livestock animals sick can also make humans ill. Meat from livestock can transmit diseases such as avian flu and mad cow disease. Chickens, cows, and pigs sometimes carry bacteria such as salmonella. Every year, 1.2 million people in the United States get sick from eating foods contaminated with salmonella. To prevent infection, many commercial livestock farmers treat their animals with antibiotics. Antibiotics are medicines that stop bacterial infections.

Some people visit Western schools to teach students about the nutrition benefits of eating bugs.

Antibiotics enter people's bodies when they eat treated meat. When antibiotics are overused, bacteria become resistant to them. The bacteria become harder to kill. Insects can also carry bacteria, parasites, and other organisms. Properly raising, storing, and cooking insects makes them safe to eat.

GOOD FOR THE ENVIRONMENT

Eating bugs does more than make bodies healthy. It is also better for the environment than raising livestock.

Insects are more sustainable. They reproduce quickly and in large numbers. They have short life spans, so they grow fast. A female house cricket, for example, lays 1,200 to 1,500 eggs in a three- or four-week period of time. At around six weeks old, crickets are large enough to be harvested.

BUGS AS ANIMAL FEED

Bugs can be used in animal feed. Protein is an expensive ingredient in foods fed to farmed animals and fish. The protein in animal feed typically comes from soy and fish meal. Growing soybeans uses land, water, and other resources. Catching fish for fish meal reduces fish populations. It also pollutes oceans. Replacing soy and fish protein with insect protein reduces costs. It is also better for the environment.

Insects use fewer resources than livestock. Bugs are efficient at turning the food they eat into body mass. They do not need much food or water because their bodies do not control their own temperature. They use less energy than warm-blooded animals to stay warm. It takes just 4.4 pounds (2 kg) of feed to make 2.2 pounds (1 kg) of edible insects. Cattle need 17.6 pounds (8 kg) of feed to gain the same weight.

Bugs also need much less water than livestock animals. Insects get most of the water they need from the food they eat. It takes 500 gallons (1,893 L) of water to make 1 pound (0.5 kg) of chicken. More than 2,000 gallons (7,571 L) of water are needed to make a pound of beef. But it takes just 1 gallon (3.8 L) of water to make a pound of crickets.

Bugs have a lower environmental impact than livestock. Insect farming does not require harmful pesticides or fertilizers. Bugs do not need land for grazing. They can be successfully raised in small spaces

PROTEIN PRODUCTION

Beef:
2,750 square
feet (255 sq m)

Mealworms:
190 square
feet (18 sq m)

The graphic below shows the amount of land used to produce 2.2 pounds (1 kg) of edible beef and mealworm protein. How many times more land is used to produce beef than mealworms?

with inexpensive materials such as bins, cardboard egg cartons, sand, and soil. Bins can be stacked vertically to use space more efficiently. Edible insects can even be raised in homes.

Another benefit of raising bugs is reduced greenhouse gas emissions. Insects do not leave behind heaps of manure. Unlike cattle and pigs, insects do not pollute land and water resources with urine. Crickets make 80 percent less methane gas than cattle.

Bugs can reduce food and agricultural wastes. When food scraps rot in landfills, they give off methane. A better alternative is to feed organic waste to insects. Food scraps and other organic waste become nutritious feed. Insect farmers can get organic waste for free or at a low cost.

FURTHER EVIDENCE

Chapter Three covers the benefits of eating insects. What was one of the main points of this chapter? What evidence is included to support this point? Read the article at the website below. Does the information on the website support the main point of the chapter? What additional information did you learn?

INSECTS – THE NEW SUPERFOOD!
abdocorelibrary.com/bugs-sustainable-food-source

THE FUTURE OF EDIBLE BUGS

E dible insects may offer food security for a growing world population. Bugs are also a sustainable source of protein. Eating insects has less of an impact on the environment than consuming livestock. While there are benefits to eating insects, there also may be potential risks. In many parts of the world, insects are usually taken from the wild. Harvesting wild insects may not be an option for long. Some insect populations are declining. In some places, too many insects are taken from the wild. Also, there are safety concerns associated with eating insects.

The popularity of some insect species as food can nearly drive them to extinction.

Pesticides and pollution contaminate insects. They harm people who eat the bugs. Insect foods may also cause allergic reactions. Eating insects is safe if they are farmed in clean facilities. Insects must be properly stored and packaged. Labels on packages warn people about allergens. And more research is needed to learn how to farm bugs in the most sustainable way.

FARMING EDIBLE BUGS

Raising edible insects in commercial farms is a more sustainable option. In Cameroon, people destroyed habitat while harvesting palm weevils in the wild. Now weevils are raised on farms. In Thailand, there are 20,000 cricket farms. The farms supply more than 8,200 tons (7,500 metric tons) of insects. Commercial farms also provide jobs for thousands of people.

Insects such as bees and silkworms are raised for products such as honey, wax, and silk. Insect farms also raise bugs to feed to pets and zoo animals. Farming insects for human food is still in its infancy. But the

People around the world are starting edible bug farms, including in Vietnam.

number of edible insect businesses is rising. So is the number of businesses that make foods using bug ingredients. People realize that edible insects are an untapped resource in parts of the world.

CHANGING ATTITUDES

Westerners have an increased interest in edible insects. But they have been slow to add bugs to their diets.

The biggest problem is the yuck factor. Some people think gobbling up whole insects is disgusting. However, people are more willing to eat bugs if they're hidden in familiar foods. Businesses are successfully selling products made from ground insects. Many people don't mind eating insect chips and granola bars. Researchers at the Eastern Shore Food Lab at Washington College in Maryland experiment with different ways of raising, harvesting, and cooking insects. They hold events such as films, lectures, and cooking contests for the public. They hope to raise awareness about the benefits of edible insects.

THE BUSINESS OF BUGS

Entomo Farms in Ontario, Canada, is the largest company farming edible insects in North America. They farm crickets and mealworms. The bugs are roasted and sold whole as snacks. Entomo also processes its bugs into powders. The powders are added to pasta, crackers, and baking mixes. Entomo provides information about what insects taste like, what their nutritional value is, and how to use them in recipes.

University students Rose Wang, Meryl Natow, and Laura D'Asaro sampled insects while abroad. They thought the insects tasted great. But more importantly, they realized that bugs are nutritious and sustainable. The team started the company Chirps. Chirps has a cricket powder, a cookie mix, and flavored tortilla chips. Chirps have less fat than potato chips. They also have more protein and other nutrients. The company founders

ROBOTIC HELPERS

Farming edible insects can be difficult. Bugs need specific conditions to survive. Temperature and humidity levels must be kept just right. Some bugs, such as crickets, only eat at night. Some farmers use technology to control growing conditions. Technology ensures that their farms are efficient and sustainable. At one Texas farm, a robot helps out. It feeds millions of crickets around the clock. Sensors monitor how the crickets feed. The robot detects when the crickets need food.

BUGS IN SPACE

Future astronauts may eat insects. NASA plans to send astronauts to Mars in the 2030s. They estimate it will take 2.5 years to travel to and from Mars. Astronauts will need nutritious food to stay healthy. Food must taste good and take up little space. It also needs to have a long shelf life. Bugs taken on previous space missions have survived and reproduced. Insects would be a good source of protein and other nutrients. They could also eat waste and make fertilizer for soil.

hope their snacks will encourage people to eat insects.

At the Audubon Butterfly Garden and Insectarium in Louisiana, visitors can look at and learn about bugs. Afterward, they can dine on Six-Legged Salsa, Hoppin' Hummus, and other insect delights at the Insectarium's Bug Appétit café. Restaurants in New York City and other major cities also have edible insects on their menus. Sweet-and-sour crickets, lime-and-salt grasshoppers, caramel mealworms, and chocolate-covered locusts

More Westerners are learning that bugs can be tasty and healthy.

are some of the offerings. These dishes give diners a chance to taste bugs in everything from appetizers to desserts. In Seattle, Washington, Mariners baseball fans happily munch on spicy grasshoppers as they cheer for their team.

FOOD OF THE FUTURE

People in Western cultures are starting to recognize the value of edible insects. But several hurdles need to be overcome before edible insects are fully accepted. Bug products are still expensive. As more edible insect businesses open, costs are expected to go down. Researchers are verifying the nutritional content of more edible insects. More people may be willing to eat insects if they know that they are a healthy food. Additional studies are essential to improve farming, harvesting, and processing. The methods must remain more sustainable than traditional meat production. As the edible insect industry grows, new guidelines are being developed. These standards ensure that edible insects and their products are safe to eat.

STRAIGHT TO THE
SOURCE

Writer Katherine Martinko explains how kids may help make edible bugs a future reality:

> *A new video . . . features people chowing down on deep-fried tarantulas in Cambodia, one crispy leg at a time. . . . The video, which was screened at the Brooklyn Bug Festival this past summer and will be shown in classrooms around the United States, is part of a push to get kids interested in eating insects.*
>
> *Why? Because marketers know that if kids can be convinced eating insects is a good idea, it bodes well for the entire edible insect industry. The younger generation will grow up into bug-eating adults, while influencing peers and family members to do the same.*

> Source: Katherine Martinko. "The Future of Edible Insects Depends on Kids," *TreeHugger*. Native Content Group, September 23, 2017. Web. Accessed November 20, 2018.

Consider Your Audience

Read this passage closely. Consider how you would adapt it for a different audience, such as your parents. Write a blog post conveying this same information for the new audience. How does your new approach differ from the original text, and why?

FAST FACTS

- Humans have been eating insects for millions of years.

- There are 2 billion people around the world who eat insects.

- Eating insects is called entomophagy.

- Most people in Western cultures think eating insects is disgusting.

- Current methods of food production will not produce enough food to feed the growing world population.

- Millions of people around the world suffer from lack of food and malnutrition.

- Land for growing crops and rearing livestock is scarce.

- Water supplies are dwindling.

- Raising livestock for meat is not sustainable.

- Edible insects are a healthier option than meat. Edible insects are high in proteins and other nutrients.

- Raising edible insects is better for the environment. They are a sustainable alternative to meat.

- Westerners are slowly accepting insects as food.

- The number of edible insect businesses is growing.

- People can eat insects in restaurants or buy snacks and other foods made with insect ingredients.

STOP AND THINK

Tell the Tale

Chapter Four describes ways that edible insects can be eaten. Imagine that you are eating insects at the Bug Appétit café or another restaurant. Write about 200 words about your dining experience. What are you eating? How does it feel? How does it taste?

Surprise Me

Chapter Two discusses how natural resources are declining. After reading this book, what two or three facts about natural resources did you find most surprising? Write a few sentences about each fact. Why did you find each fact surprising?

Dig Deeper

After reading this book, what questions do you still have about edible insects? With an adult's help, find a few reliable sources that can help you answer your questions. Write a paragraph about what you learned.

You Are There

This book discusses insect farming. Imagine you are working at an insect farm. Write a letter home telling your friends what the farm is like. Describe what you do to care for the insects. Be sure to add plenty of detail to your notes.

GLOSSARY

contaminated
having picked up substances
that are unwanted or harmful

edible
safe to be eaten

emit
to give off

entomophagist
a person who eats insects

extinction
the dying out of a group of
animals or plants

larva
a caterpillar or grub form of
an insect

livestock
farm animals such as
chickens, pigs, and cattle

malnutrition
a sickness caused by not
eating enough of the
nutrients and foods the
body needs

manure
body waste produced
by animals

nutritious
food that helps a person
grow and stay healthy

pesticide
a substance that kills insects

pollution
harmful things that cause
damage in an environment

sustainable
not using up
natural resources

ONLINE
RESOURCES

To learn more about eating bugs as sustainable food, visit our free resource websites below.

Core Library
CONNECTION
FREE! COMMON CORE MULTIMEDIA RESOURCES

Visit **abdocorelibrary.com** or scan this QR code for free Common Core resources for teachers and students, including vetted activities, multimedia, and booklinks, for deeper subject comprehension.

Booklinks
NONFICTION NETWORK
FREE! ONLINE NONFICTION RESOURCES

Visit **abdobooklinks.com** or scan this QR code for free additional online weblinks for further learning. These links are routinely monitored and updated to provide the most current information available.

LEARN
MORE

Felix, Rebecca. *Eating Ethically*. Minneapolis, MN: Abdo Publishing, 2016. Print.

Hamilton, S. L. *Beetles*. Minneapolis, MN: Abdo Publishing, 2015. Print.

INDEX

About the Author

Cecilia Pinto McCarthy has written several books for children and teens about science, nature, and technology. She also teaches classes at a nature sanctuary. She and her family live north of Boston, Massachusetts.